Bucket List Living
For Moms

Become a More Adventurous
Parent

Lara Krupicka

Bucket List Living For Moms
Copyright © 2014 Lara Krupicka

Cover image by Steve Cole Images
Cover design by Jason Katz
Author photo by Emily Neal

Wordcrafter Communications
1119 Sara Ln., Naperville, IL 60565

ISBN: 978-0-9912627-2-4

1. Parenting & Relationships. 2. Motherhood. I. Title.

This book is dedicated to my mom, Mary Seman, whose sense of enjoyment & adventure inspires me to this day. So many times in my own parenting, my memories of the goofy, light-hearted things she did in my childhood remind me to lighten up. And I'm grateful for the encouragement she's given me toward living out my personal dreams and goals.

Find many more great bucket list resources at www.larakrupicka.com.

Table of Contents

Introduction: Become a More Adventurous Parent 5

How to Use This Book 9

Your "Done It" List 11

Your Hopes Now 19

Your Goals Before Kids 29

A Bucket List Draft 39

A List to Display.. 43

Kids, Bucket Lists & Bonding.. 45

Common Challenges.. 49

Adventure Commemoration 55

Conclusion: Embracing the Bucket List Life 61

Save Idea Lists For Later... 63

Digital Tools 65

The Bucket List Life Manifesto...................................... 67

About the Author 69

An Invitation to Connect 71

Check Out *Family Bucket Lists* 73

Introduction:
Become a More Adventurous Parent

Have you ever hung out with a group of moms and been surprised to learn of the lives these women led before kids? You never knew the Girl Scout troop leader was once a CEO. Or that your carpool buddy played on a championship college volleyball team. Perhaps you have surprised other moms when you shared certain parts of your life history.

Moms are some pretty amazing people. But while it is refreshing to see how motherhood levels the playing field, there is a danger. That danger is the stifling of your personal identity under the heavy mantle of motherhood. You can only sacrifice for the little people in your life for so long before you begin to forget who you were... or who you are.

The good news is that it is not only fun and easy to rediscover yourself, it is also beneficial to the role you play as a mom.

Do you remember how it felt when you went after a goal in life? When you promised yourself you would do that one thing you had always wanted to do or visit that place or meet that favorite celebrity? And do you remember how it thrilled you to get up each day with the thought of gaining more ground on that goal?

That is what this book invites you to. A space where you can honor those pursuits that set your insides buzzing. A chance to explore and reconnect with the person you have become in the years since you gave birth or adopted your first child. A time to refuel yourself through deeply personal interests, so that you are better equipped to pour into your family.

Bucket list living as a mom is a great experience. The world that shrunk to the four walls of your home will expand once again as you reach out toward your goals. Your relationship with your kids will take on new dimensions with you being the one to explore and grow on occasion. And the perspective you have gained through parenting will enrich and inform your adventures in unique ways to make them more powerful for you, your family, and those whose paths you cross along the way.

You will be surprised at how many opportunities exist today for you to go after your life dreams. Our culture offers us so much more access to people and resources, particularly via the Internet, that allow us to move forward without even leaving home. This is great news for us moms, who often have to filter time for ourselves and our interests into the minutes available in our busy family lives. And you'll find this paradox at work: often the more you invest in yourself, the more personal resources (time, finances, energy) become available to you for investing further.

You need to live your bucket list dreams and be true to all of who you are. Your kids need you to be a mom who knows where she is headed and delights to have them along for the journey. The world needs you to pursue what you've been made to do. Anything less short-changes us all.

So get ready for the adventure of living out your dreams. As I say in the Bucket List Life Manifesto: "plan to amaze yourself."

How to Use This Book

Bucket List Living for Moms is designed to propel you right into the heart of recalling (and discovering) your life dreams and then making them happen.

The first few chapters provide questions about the types of activities, places, and people that are significant to you as a means to explore options for populating your bucket list. Each chapter stands on its own, which means you can flip back and forth between the exercises in each just as easily as going straight through them in order. You could take the questions quickly to capture the first response that comes to mind. Or you could dive deep and journal at length about the thoughts, memories and feelings that arise. Whatever method you choose, I hope you find the process fun and enlightening.

The next two chapters offer suggestions for how to organize and display your list. These are meant to help you end up with a list in a form that most inspires you to action. You could follow the suggestions exactly as written. Or play around to come up with a form uniquely your own.

Following that you will find tips and inspiration on how to mesh a bucket list life with raising kids. My goal is that this section will show you that the bucket list life is not only doable as a mom, but preferable. You could use the information here to prepare for the adventures ahead. Or refer back to it once you are living your dreams as a touchstone and guide.

The beauty of bucket lists is that just as they represent us and our dreams, like us they also grow and change. You will be surprised once you have begun the bucket list journey at how opportunities spring up around you. New ideas beg to be added to your list. Even the act of completing a bucket list goal can be the source of further exploration. Some of your answers to the questions in this book five years from now will be quite different from those at present.

I hope you will return to this book throughout your journey.

Your "Done It" List

What once-in-a-lifetime experiences have you had so far? No doubt you have not reached this point in your life without seeing or doing things that dazzled, surprised and fulfilled you. After all, you did become a mom.

Normally we think of those experiences yet to come when we envision our bucket list. But you stand to gain a certain energy by considering the paths you have already traveled. When you compress all of the years and all of the experiences in your life into one list it can be awe-inspiring.

When I look back on what I have learned, roles I have filled and places I have traveled, it stirs me. I will never break a record in sprinting again, but I wonder what my body would be capable of with some training now. I once was daring enough to travel across the globe on my own – certainly I can dare a few new things. Those reflections on my past experiences motivate me to move toward my next goal.

The same can be true for you. I am guessing you have interesting stories you could tell about your life thus far. Start your bucket list journey by reviewing where you have been.

You may want to pull out old scrapbooks, memorabilia,

or photo albums to jog your memory. Settle in somewhere quiet (maybe with your favorite drink and snack). Then answer the following series of questions to collect your bucket list memories:

Self-improvement/Pushing Your Own Limits

As a youth, what sports did you enjoy? Can you remember any personal bests from your youth sports days? Did you receive any recognition athletically?

Can you recall any performance highlights – musical, theatre, or otherwise from your childhood? High school years? College? Beyond college?

What hobbies did you have as a child? As a teen? In your college and/or single years?

What stands out in your memory as something you did well in high school or college?

As a kid did you ever teach yourself how to do something exceptionally tricky or challenging? Or did you have a special ability that no one else did?

In your school years what achievement were you most proud of?

Have you ever done something that defied your fears?

What else have you accomplished that you thought you would never do?

The World at Large

What were the most memorable trips you took as a child?

Did you take any school trips as a junior high or high school student – locally or abroad?

What places, such as museums, left an impression on you?

Where, besides your current home, have you lived before?

Where did you and your spouse honeymoon?

Have you taken any special trips, just you and your husband, since your honeymoon?

Did you ever take a road trip with friends?

Social/Emotional Goals
Have you ever met someone famous? Inspiring? Who?

What concerts did you go to as a teen? In college? Before you had kids?

What jobs have you held in the past?

Can you think of a time in your youth when you made a difference in someone else's life?

Do you have particular relational skills that showed up when you were young – compassion, extraordinary generosity, sensitivity, kindheartedness?

What roles have you held in organizations you have belonged to?

Have you known someone who went on to attain notoriety?

What unexpected or otherwise surprising role or job or position or persona have you held in your life thus far?

Whimsy

Name something crazy you did as a kid.

What goofy escapades did you get into as a high schooler?

List any pranks or jokes you pulled or stunts you were involved in as a college student.

I hope some amusing times and remarkable stories came to mind as you went through these questions. Are any of those stories ones you want to pass along to future generations? If you haven't chronicled them elsewhere before – in a photo album, journal or other form – consider whether this is a project you want to undertake. You could choose to make that a task for now. Or, knowing you have notes about them in your responses to these exercises, you could proceed to the next part in the bucket list making process: recording your current hopes.

Your Hopes Now

When you think "bucket list," what comes to mind?

Places you would like to go?

Everyone has a wish list of places they would like to travel. Unless you write down your dream destinations before you add other ideas to your bucket list, your travel fantasies are going to stand in the way of other possibilities.

Here you can write down all the places in the world, near and far, you would like to visit in your lifetime. If there are spots you have already been to, but you are hoping to take your spouse or kids for the first time, make sure you capture those too.

Go ahead and create a list called "Places I Want to Visit in My Lifetime."

Did you record them all?

Great. You have freed your mind to move on to the less travel-oriented aspects of your bucket list. The locations you want to visit are only a part of your list.

The questions below should help you recover or discover any "someday" goals you have considered in the years since you became a mom.

Self-improvement/Pushing Your Own Limits

Has anything already come to mind of something you want to do for yourself? Write it down here.

Have you ever wanted to pursue an activity or enter a competition that pushes the limits of your body? List it here.

What long-held fear would you like to push past? What goal would enable you to face it head on?

Have you ever considered entering a competition that would allow you to test the limits of your talents or skills? What competition(s)?

List one thing you believe would be very cool to say you have done, but that you are not sure you are capable of doing right now.

Name something you have always wanted to learn how to do, but have not yet.

Is there a particular class you have wanted to take, a subject you want to explore or a hobby you would like to try?

How do you dream of spending your retirement years, in terms of what you will be doing with your time?

Have you considered a second career or change in career as your children become older? What shape would you like your future career to take?

If money, connections, experience, or talent were no object, what would be your ideal job? Or how would you spend your day?

The World at Large

You have already listed places you want to visit. But I am guessing you have more you want to explore in this world. If anything new has come to mind of where you want to go, jot it here:

Name any museums you have always wanted to see.

What city/cities have you dreamed of exploring?

Is there a national park, beach or other destination that should be on your list of places to explore one day?

How about restaurants, nearby or far away, you have been meaning to check out?

In addition to those particular restaurants, list any types of foods you want to try, be it a category like an ethnic variety, or a specific dish.

Have you ever dreamed of living somewhere else one day? A specific location? Type of home?

Is there an upcoming history-making event you would like to witness?

Social/Emotional Goals

Is there someone who shares one of your life goals that might want to join you in completing it? Write down who and what that is for any goals here.

Describe your idea of the ideal girlfriend getaway. Do not be afraid to list more than one, if you have multiple groups of friends you want to hang out with in different settings.

Name a famous/inspirational person you would want to sit down to dinner with.

Whose work or lifestyle have you admired from afar?

Is there someone whose opinion or mindset you would love to learn one-on-one?

Who else would you like to meet, even briefly?

What live performance(s) you would like to experience – theatre, concert, comedian, etc.?

Describe the perfect date night or romantic escape you would like to share with your husband or significant other.

Is there a compilation you have wanted to create for your children to have in the future – a recipe book, family history, heirloom, recording?

Whimsy

What crazy escapade would you like to undertake someday – something outlandish, silly or otherwise out of character for you?

Name a place you would like to visit "just because."

Name a dare you have been wanting to take.

So far, so good. By now your mind should be attuned to those once-in-a-lifetime pursuits that pique your interest. Do not be surprised if bucket list ideas continue to spring up over the coming days and weeks. Be prepared to jot them down as they occur and incorporate them into those you have already noted.

Your list should not end there though. If you are ready, there are more exercises to complete.

Your Goals Before Kids

You have considered your accomplishments and life experiences to date. And you thought through the wishes you have right now for what you want to see and do and be. But if you are like me, there is more to your bucket list. There are goals you pushed aside in adulthood to make room for "real life." And there are hopes you held in younger years that you completely forgot about.

I often find random situations will surface a memory of a childhood wish. Whenever I spot a box of Café du Monde beignet mix in the grocery store, I immediately recall growing up eating the puffy powdered-sugar-coated donuts my mom made with the mix she mail ordered from the iconic New Orleans' café. And my old longing to visit the café to try hot beignets fresh from the source springs up again. A trip to Café du Monde is on my bucket list.

You probably have those experiences too. But why not see how many of those old longings you can recall right now? Roll up your sleeves for some time-travel fun. You are going to look at the types of activities and experiences that thrilled you as a child. In doing so, you may discover clues concerning what you had hoped to do before becoming a mom that you have not yet accomplished.

Self-improvement/Pushing Your Own Limits

Did you ever set any goals in sports before you were married that you didn't reach?

What physical skills or activities did you enjoy as a child or teen? Did you ever envision those abilities playing a significant role in your life or enabling a particular accomplishment?

What else did you show ability or interest in as a child that you did not carry into motherhood? Would it be worth dabbling in again – either by taking classes or simply re-engaging as a hobby?

What did others praise you for as a teen? As a child? Do those skills or traits lend themselves to a larger aim you might consider?

As a child, what did you dream of becoming when you grew up? Did the answer change over time? List as many roles as you can remember. Did you fill any of those roles?

Was there a skill, sport or physical feat you wanted to master as a child but never did? Was it due to lack of ability, practice, training, resources (money) or some combination of these things?

In your childhood, was there an experience you hoped to have that never came to be?

Is there someone you would have liked to share a special experience with? If it is not possible to share this with them today, would taking part in the experience honor that person's memory in some way?

How did you most like to spend free time before kids that you do not engage in now? Is this something you miss and might return to one day?

The World at Large

When you and your husband first wed, where did you talk of traveling together that you have not yet gone?

What place did you wish to go to most when you were a kid? Did you ever get there? If so, would it be worth returning to?

When you were young, what sort of place did you dream of living in? Was it a particular location or type of home? Have you lived in a place like that since childhood? If not, is it a location or place where you could rent a home for a brief time to experience what it would be like?

Did you have a special location you liked to visit as a child? A vacation spot? Someone's house? Would you like to go there again in the future?

What would have been your ideal "road trip" or spring break destination as a teen or college student? What made it ideal to you then? Would it still be ideal to you now?

Was there an artifact or artwork you would have loved to view up close, but missed?

Social/Emotional Goals

Did you have a hero as a teen? What made you look up to them?

Is there someone from your past whom you would like to thank or otherwise pay tribute to for the influence they played in your life – a teacher, friend, clergy person, boss, parent?

Whom did you hope to be like when you grew up?

Do you remember stories told in your family when you were young that were special to you? Is there someone still living who could retell the stories to you or record them for you in some form – written, audio, video?

What athlete, movie star, author, musician, dignitary, or other celebrity would you have loved to meet as a child? List as many names as you can remember (even if they are not living).

What food from your childhood have you not eaten in a long time that you most miss? Is there any way to taste it again? If it is home cooked, can you seek out the recipe?

Name an individual (or group) you were crazy about as a teen.

Name an expert who inspired teenaged/young adult you. What did they do so well that impressed you?

Is there a person who stands out in your memory as having influenced you from afar in your pre-kids years?

What celebrity was popular before you had kids that you would have liked to meet?

Whimsy

Did you ever talk of creating or doing something that seemed like a stretch when you were young?

What silly thing did you talk about doing as a teen, but never did? Would you consider doing it now?

What outlandish experience were you denied as a child (by circumstance, finances, location or otherwise)?

It's nostalgic to reflect on where you projected yourself going in life. To recall the youthful, expectant version of yourself to whom the whole world represented grand possibility. The good news is you can still follow some of those paths you envisioned in your youth – or at least a modified version of them. You ought to include on your bucket list as many of your long-held dreams as possible.

I have found achieving bucket list goals that string back to my childhood to be some of my most touching experiences. For example, not long ago I had the unexpected chance to sit down at lunch with David Newell, the actor who played Mr. McFeely in the children's television show Mr. Rogers' Neighborhood. As a child I watched the show often and Mr. McFeely was my favorite character. It had not occurred to me one day I would be chatting with him face-to-face. Yet at the end of our time together when he sent me off with his trademark farewell of "Speedy Delivery!" my spirits soared.

My hope for you, having completed the questions in this book, is that you will have unearthed ideas and plans that will yield the same childlike surprise and joy. And that you will have connected with hopes whose completion will be infinitely meaningful.

A Bucket List Draft

You have done a lot of work to this point. Fun work loaded with self-discovery and memory collecting. Your bucket list is taking shape. Your answers from the previous chapters contain what you need to draft a list you will be eager to complete.

Do not stop now. You will give yourself the best chance at doing all you hope to do by writing them in a list of goals for yourself. Researcher Dr. Gail Matthews of Dominican University in California discovered that:

- Just writing down a goal, versus merely thinking of one, provided significantly greater success (between 33-50% more achieved).
- Writing down a goal and sharing it with a friend accomplished more than the act of writing it down alone.
- Writing down a goal, sharing it with a friend, and then checking in regularly about progress toward the goal elicited noticeably higher levels of achievement than writing and sharing the goal without regular accountability.

As women, we have the whole sharing with a friend thing locked up, right? I imagine you could find a friend whom you could check in with about your bucket list. The hardest part might be getting the list in writing. And you are going to do that part now.

Your list does not have to be pretty at this point; it simply needs to be written down. Here is the most straight-forward method for creating your list, using the work you have already done:

- Go back to your notes from chapter two. Copy down all of your "Self-improvement/Pushing Your Own Limits" goals onto a list. Then find all of the answers from chapter three in that same category. If you want to keep your "done it" list alongside your future goals, do the same with your answers from chapter one.

- Now gather your answers under "The World at Large" category from the previous chapters.

- Then go back through to find your "Social/Emotional Goals" from the beginning exercises.

- Finally, collect everything you listed under "Whimsy."

If you want to compile the four categories into one page, you can download the free chart "My Bucket List" from my website, www.larakrupicka.com.

You may also want to include your "Places I Want to

Visit in My Lifetime" from chapter one.

Another way to organize your life longings is as a "Top 10" list or series of such lists. If that appeals to you, take a crack at any or all of the following (incorporating answers from the previous chapters and any new ideas that come up):

Top 10 Places I Want to Visit

Top 10 People I Want to Meet

Top 10 Things I Want to Learn

Top 10 Foods or Restaurants I Want to Try

Top 10 Shows/Concerts/Movies I Want to See

Top 10 Activities I Want to Experience

Create your own Top 10 related to one of your interests (Top 10 Spas to Visit, Top 10 Golf Courses to Play, Top 10 Wines to Sample, Top 10 Rock Climbs to Conquer, etc.). This is a great method for listing sub-categories. You are only limited by your imagination (which I hope is becoming more expansive through these exercises).

Additional methods include writing one long list on loose-leaf paper or a pocket notepad or dictating it to your smart phone or laptop. Try typing it into a spreadsheet or word processing document. Use whatever method and whatever organizational format works to create a list that makes sense to you.

Have fun creating your bucket list draft (or drafts). After all, you are giving yourself goals that will extend across the rest of your life. And the beauty of it is, you will continue to expand that list as one experience inspires another and old ideas continue to come to mind.

A List to Display

Look at that! You have a bucket list. You have written down what you want to make happen in your lifetime.

Your list reveals your personality – your interests, your quirks, your God-given passions and your talents. It springs from your life experiences, your innermost ambitions, and your childhood longings. Just as all of those pieces are unique to you, so your bucket list is unique. Your list will not match mine, nor will it match your best friend's, even if there is some overlap.

How you choose to display the finished version of your list will differ also. It can be a reflection of your personality, be it fancy, avant-garde or straight up simple. So consider where and how you want to display your list and what you want it to look like. What visual form can your list take that will inspire you most?

Here are some display ideas for you to consider:

- Written on a large chalkboard or dry erase board (which everyone agrees not to erase).

- On a wall map, with tags marking places where your adventures will take place.

- Framed and hung in your office or kitchen.

- Printed up as a subway art poster or wall decoration.

- Created as a word cloud using a site like Wordle and the resulting image printed on canvas.

- Mounted on individual cards decorated with scrapbook paper, and pinned to a bulletin board.

- Written with a Sharpie onto wooden clothespins and clipped around the edge of an actual bucket or onto a clothesline.

- Gathered as a collage of tagged photos representing each of your goals.

- Printed on strips of colorful paper taped into loops and strung together as a chain to drape around a doorframe.

However you decide to display your bucket list, what is most important is that you see it regularly, even if you simply print it out and tape it to the inside of your bathroom cabinet or daily planner. You took the effort to capture a bucket list. Now you deserve to capitalize on the inspiration it can bring you and the success that research shows comes from regularly reviewing your goals.

Kids, Bucket Lists & Bonding

Do you want to grow persistent kids? Show persistence.

Do you want to grow fearless kids? Be fearless.

Because they happen outside the realm of ordinary life, your bucket list experiences provide opportunities to model the type of character you want to instill in your kids. But better still, your experiences provide a source of bonding.

I remember the first time I tried archery. My youngest daughter had wanted to give it a shot. During a camping trip the park rangers announced an archery clinic for kids. I went along to watch, wishing I could try it too. When the instructor saw my eagerness, she made a spot for me and coached me in taking a few shots. My aim was worse than that of my daughter, who seemed to have an affinity for the sport.

Afterward we swapped frustrations about how difficult archery is. My daughter offered a few pointers with great sympathy for my lack of skill. I was touched by her attentiveness and desire to see me succeed.

In parenting, those role reversals are rare. But when they happen, they make a big difference in the parent-child relationship. Instead of focusing on always getting behind your kids' endeavors, make sure you weave in opportunities for your kids to support you. In fact, the more often you do so, the more growth you, your child, and your relationship will experience. Your bucket list goals provide a prime source for these interactions.

The joy of reaching a big goal is fantastic. Sharing that joy with your kids can make it even better. And your kids will want to share in your bucket list experiences, whether they accompany you or hear about it in your stories afterward. There is something about taking life by the collar that can bring parents and kids together in unique and satisfying ways. Do not miss that benefit to bucket list living as a mom.

Here are some ways you can use your bucket list and the growth it brings to draw closer to your children:

- Share your fears as you approach a new bucket list experience. Explain to your child what you plan to do to overcome those fears. Afterward, discuss how your strategy succeeded (or failed) in aiding you. In future days point out when you notice how that bucket list venture made a permanent change in your attitude toward something that previously scared you.

- Invite your child to join you in checking off a bucket list item when possible, especially when it is a dream on both of your lists. You will find doing so momentarily levels the playing field. Yes, you are still mother and child. But you are also fellow explorers venturing into new territory. You will be nervous together. Or awestruck. Or elated. Side by side.

- Let your child cheer you on toward an aspiration. Often as parents we live on the sidelines. It can be eye opening for kids to watch as a parent embraces an experience. They will enjoy the chance to be the one on the sidelines for a change. And you will find your enthusiasm buoyed by their support.

- When you struggle to learn a new skill or find a way through bucket list challenges, avoid the temptation to always conceal those struggles. It can help your child to see that you face challenges too. Just as you did with your fears, demonstrate to your child the strategies you use to work through your struggles.

- When you struggle, also consider asking your child for input and insight. Remember that kids do not have the same filters and have not been boxed in by expectations the way we have. So your child might see a solution you cannot. Imagine what it will do for both of you and the way you relate, for you to receive help from your child this way.

- Draw on your bucket list experiences to express empathy when your child faces a new experience (for a great animated illustration of empathy suitable for both adults and kids, check out Dr. Brene Brown's video clip by The RSA on YouTube, called The Power of Empathy). This emotion enables you to come alongside your child and relate human to human, rather than parent to child. Thank your bucket list for allowing you to stretch outside your comfort zone, just like kids are forced to do regularly by the nature of being a kid.

Include your kids in your bucket list adventures in as many different ways as you can. You will see the positive impacts on your relationship for years to come.

Common Challenges

Bucket lists can be inspiring. But finding ways to cross off even one item can bring plenty of frustration – especially for those of us in the midst of raising children. It helps to know that challenges will arise. Then, instead of ditching your list or assuming you will wait until your children are grown, take a deep breath. Remember that bucket list hopes worth pursuing are worth the effort to reach.

Recognize that unless you value your dreams, no one else will. Address the challenges you face. Whittle away at them until you find yourself launching into dream after dream. You will have much to be proud of, not the least of which is the model you have set for your children for overcoming obstacles in the name of that which matters most.

Here are suggestions for how to prevail over some of the most common challenges moms face on their journey to living out their bucket lists:

Lack of time

- Share the family time budget. Take a turn being the one to sign up for a class or activity.

- Share the workload. Delegate some of your household responsibilities to other family members during the time you'll be engaged in your pursuit. This is a win-win-win. Your kids gain life skills. You are enabled to carry out a goal you want to fulfill. Your family gains a mom who is more inspired, more fulfilled, more fit, more...fill in the blank with how you'll be improved through your time.

- Trade childcare with another mom friend. One week she spends an afternoon on her goals while you hang with the kids. The next week it is your turn to be kid-free. Do this during the day if you are a stay-at-home mom with young ones, or after school if your kiddos are older.

- Find family-friendly activities. Instead of learning Irish step dancing alone, take the parent-child class. You get to share the experience and your child learns along with you. Look for opportunities to go together instead of splitting up and heading different directions.

- Chunk your activities to free up time. Rather than run errands on multiple days, make one day errand day. Spend another day only on household chores. Then designate a few hours one day for your special "me" time.

- Swap out other activities. Decide if there is an existing use of your time that you can sacrifice to focus on progress toward a bucket list goal. Wake up early to work on the novel you always wanted to write. Switch from working out at a gym to training with future marathoners.

- Use the drive time to listen and learn. Grab audiobooks related to one of your bucket list interests – a language course, travel guide, or instructional book. Turn it on in the carpool lane and any other time you drive sans kids (or even when they are present if the topic suits them too).

Lack of support

- Do it for yourself. When you are following what most interests you, you need to draw on your own internal motivation to keep going. Remind yourself of why you listed the things you did.

- Seek out like-minded people. Find a friend who has the same goal on her bucket list and go after it together. Join a club or organization for people who share one of your interests.

- Listen to your cheerleaders. Tune out the negative. Tune in the positive.

- Ask for what you need. Sometimes family members may not understand what you are looking for from them. Tell them in clear terms what it would look like for them to show support.

- Train your children to be supportive – of you and of each other. Explain how you show them support and ask them to do the same. Model supportiveness, then practice it together.

- Try, try again. Pick a different ambition that better suits your family at this time.

Lack of finances

- Start with research. It costs nothing to look into the details of making a dream come true. In fact, a bit of legwork ahead of time often saves money. Gathering information also provides a sense of progress. You are that much closer to making it happen.

- Think small. Choose your least expensive goal to save toward first. Again, being able to check something off the list without a long wait can be inspiring.

- Watch deal-aggregators such as Groupon and LivingSocial for discounts on bucket list pursuits. A recent look at one Groupon email revealed options for ski lift tickets, a pottery-throwing class and sushi meal all for less than $30 apiece.

- Team up with others to split the cost of equipment, rentals, and other big overhead expenses.

- Sacrifice for the cause. Give up movie night once

a month or your daily trip to the coffee shop. Put the savings into a bucket list account.

- Hold a "bucket list dream" garage sale or create a Craigslist, bookoo or other online secondhand sales account to sell from. Then purge your closet and crawlspace of belongings you no longer need. Earmark the earnings for a bucket list experience.

- Use the barter system. You may need to get creative about it, but swap your know-how with someone who holds the keys to a bucket list experience.

Imagine the satisfaction of completing a goal in spite of the obstacles. Press in. Learn. Be creative. You have it in you to make your longings a reality. The roadblocks will make the success that much sweeter.

Adventure Commemoration

Look again at your bucket list. Are you excited yet about all you are going to see and do in the coming months and years? Imagine the stories you will have to tell. You will want to have evidence of it all. You will want to capture those once-in-a-lifetime events for the future to remember and share. Now is the time to imagine what shape those commemorations may take.

The number of forms your commemoration could take is only limited by your own creativity. You may find that you use several different types, depending on the experience being captured. Let me offer you my favorite quick-and-easy suggestions.

Top 10 Bucket List Commemorations for Busy Moms:

1. Shadow box
If you have gathered a variety of related objects and you want to exhibit them together, consider using a shadow box. This three-dimensional frame gives you space to tell a story with those objects. Then they can be put on display while being protected from damage. A series of shadow boxes can track your adventures over time.

2. Collection
Ticket stubs and theatre bills. Plates, thimbles, charms. Concert t-shirts. Race bibs. Postcards. If you like to bring

home bits and pieces from your travels and bucket list events, you may find them taking a theme that comes together as a collection. Some people like to be intentional about purchasing or saving a certain type of object in every place they travel or every event they attend. Watch your tastes and see if similar items keep coming home with you that you can eventually assemble into a collection to display.

3. Map

A large wall map pocked with pushpins can document your bucket list travels. And it can also note the places where memorable events occurred. If you like anchoring your stories on the sites where they took place, this could be a powerful visual for capturing your bucket list. Add a note beside each pin to describe what it represents. Or mat a photograph with a map of the location where it took place, and then display multiple maps and photos as a group.

The Google Maps site has the capability of creating the same type of display in digital form. Simply generate a custom map, including digital photos or YouTube videos using the "create map" button under "My Places" on maps.google.com.

4. Calendar

At the end of a calendar year you may decide to toss your regular wall calendar into your memento bin as an easy reference to what happened that year. Or you can buy a calendar that you keep separate and use only to record special events and adventures (and not for daily appointments and schedules).

To observe a year of adventures remembered, put together a photo calendar using an online photo service. Feature photos of favorite bucket list memories each month as inspiration for what you will do throughout the year as you continue living the bucket list lifestyle.

5. Photobook
If you primarily record your accomplishments through photographs, you may want to consider compiling them in a photobook. Unlike a scrapbook, with many layers, lots of glue, and potentially delicate pieces, a printed photobook can provide you with a coffee-table-quality book that highlights the images and stories of your adventures. The disadvantage of a photobook over a scrapbook is that the book needs to be completed before you can have it printed (and thus is not as accessible an option for an ongoing compilation). But the results can be impressive, making it worthwhile when you have accumulated a book's worth of memories. You can also keep an ongoing bucket list compilation through a series of photobooks.

6. Hat/shirt/canvas bag/autograph book
Remember autograph books? They still make them (just watch the crowds at Disney World to see children carrying Disney's commercial version). But you could also designate a regular notebook or journal for capturing the signatures of noteworthy people you meet. Leave facing pages blank for inserting a photograph, if you would like. Or you may prefer to be spontaneous and

catch a signature on whatever you have with you at the moment, such as an article of clothing. Then you have the option of continuing to wear the item or display it on a wall.

7. Jewelry
Charm bracelets have long been used to mark milestones. Thanks to a resurgence in popularity, it is becoming easier again to find charms. You can also use lockets to tuck memorabilia into, with one or two chains sporting multiple lockets. Consider whether jewelry could be a beautiful, wearable representation of your achievements.

8. Memory jars
Using glass jars, you can contain and display tokens from your bucket list adventures (such as layers of sand from each beach you visit, or rocks collected from different locations and labeled with a memory). Try using a variety of shapes, sizes and colors of clear or opaque jars to create interest within your display. For jars with wider mouths you can insert a corresponding photo as a backdrop to the objects. If you like, create labels for the jars themselves to mark the contents.

9. Sports gear or supplies used in activities
Mount on a wall the shoes from that marathon you ran. Glue the golf ball from your first hole-in-one on a mounted tee. Be creative with displaying items used in the consummation of special life goals as a commemoration.

10. Plastic storage container
You could choose to simply leave everything in a box, so the items can be taken out and handled, if this is what you prefer. In this case, you may wish to use clear, see-through tubs, which invite more interaction than opaque boxes might. For future reference, you may want to tag each item, noting its significance in order to recall exactly where it is from and what it represents.

I provide examples of many of these ideas (and more) on my Pinterest Board (amusingmomlara), along with links to vendors selling journals, scrapbooks and other supplies.

Whether you use one, two or many of these methods of commemorating your achievements, remember to enjoy the process. Then celebrate your achievements over and over each time you see those commemorative items. Because while those achievements happen only once, you can continue to revel in them with the reminders you create. And those reminders can stimulate you to move forward toward other goals.

So while the commemoration of a bucket list event may seem like the end, it is only part of the cycle of living out your bucket list, one goal at a time, over and over across your lifetime.

Conclusion:
Embracing the Bucket List Life

I hope throughout the course of reading this book and completing the exercises you have built a new enthusiasm for life. Your life. You have much to offer the world as you head out to see, do, be, and meet all that is on your bucket list.

Imagine what your family life will be like as you engage in what matters most – engagement within your family and for your family, and out in the world for yourself and others. The example you set for your kids of being vitally involved in life, continually learning and experiencing is priceless.

You will have the benefit of any one or more of the following as a mom:

- Greater fulfillment

- Increased capacity to relate to your children's struggles as they venture into new territory.

- A more carefree attitude toward life and the ability to capture the whimsy in situations.

- A sense of daring.

- Improved inner strength and perseverance.

- Broader sense of purpose.

- Closer relationship with your family.

- Deeper connection to the world beyond your doorstep.

Enjoy the adventure of being a mom and an explorer. Savor the journey with your family and in your own right. Embrace the bucket list life!

Appendix:

Save Idea Lists For Later

You may have noticed that I did not provide you with any sample bucket lists in this book. The reason is simple: I want you to end up with the absolute best, most authentic and most inspiring list you can create. Research shows that examples and idea lists stifle that, a psychological effect called inhibition.

Sendhil Mullainathan and Eldar Shafir, authors of the book, *Scarcity: Why Having Too Little Means So Much* give an example of the inhibition effect using the task of naming things that are white. After asking the reader to list as many as possible, Mullainathan & Shafir suggest that it would not have helped had they offered examples such as "milk" and "snow." According to the authors, "in experiments, people given these 'helpers' name fewer total items, even counting the freebies."

The same can happen with bucket lists. It is why the most common answers to the bucket list question relate to travel. Our concept of bucket lists has been narrowed by previous experiences with listing vacation goals.

Once you have had the opportunity to create a great list on your own *then* visit bucket list sites, check out books on 1001 things to do before you die, or pin one of the many bucket list images out there. When you have a complete original bucket list, then you also have a perspective on which of those 1,001 things or gazillion pins are worthy of adding to your list (and ultimately, your life).

Idea lists can be good for jogging your memory. Many times I have read another person's list and thought, "That is right, I have always wanted to do that," in response to a goal on their list. So do not be afraid to skim existing bucket lists for inspiration.

Idea lists can also be good for fleshing out a dream. If your goal is to test the limits of your body by becoming a marathoner, then you may want to look at a list of the top marathons to run in your lifetime. When planning a trip to a dream destination, it would serve you well to research the not-to-miss activities and stops related to the place you are headed.

Have fun perusing the myriad of bucket lists and bucket list images out there. Hopefully they will make you more enthused about going after your own goals.

Digital Tools

If you are digitally minded, you may find yourself drawn to using a digital tool for keeping and tracking your bucket list. There are dozens of free websites and apps dedicated to this purpose. Many of them also link in social media to enable you to share with your friends and followers and tap into the power of networking to achieve your goals. Note that every site or app will require you to create an account to make use of its features.

In reading this book, you already have completed the first step necessary for using one of these sites or apps: assembling your bucket list. Almost all of the digital tools assume you have at least the start of a bucket list. A few offer rudimentary idea-starters that may hinder, rather than encourage the process (as I mentioned in the previous section). You will be in good shape to take advantage of what these tools offer by having worked through the bucket list exercises in this book.

On my website, larakrupicka.com, I share a long list of bucket list tools, including nearly 40 websites and apps. While many have similar features, not all are created equal. Here are some of the features that make the better ones stand out:

- Simple-to-use list creation and achievement record tools.
- Widgets for posting your bucket list to your website or blog

- "What inspired you" prompts for each of your bucket list entries to help you work toward getting to a more personal, meaningful reason for pursuing them.
- Sharp photo representations for list ideas, with the option to add any of those ideas to your list by the click of a button.
- Features to cheer and comment on individual goals that allow members to interact in methods reminiscent of popular social media sites.
- "Unlock achievement" features to build up credit for your bucket list achievements giving a multi-player-online-role-playing-game feel where members can collaborate with others to reach their goals.
- Mobile device versions to track your list and achievements on the fly.
- Online map-based layouts that give you the option to find geographically located bucket list activities via map pins – great for vacation planning.

Once you have test driven one or two tools you will have a better feel for how you want your digital list to function for you. I encourage you to check out my resource list online to learn about the tools available – along with my list of books and magazines that can encourage you to make the most of bucket list living. I regularly update these lists as new apps and websites launch and old ones are updated with new features, and as I discover new books.

The Bucket List Life Manifesto

Shortly after I began championing bucket lists in earnest, I drafted a charge to those going after their life goals. I wanted to offer encouragement and a set of parameters that would spur others on to a lifestyle that makes the world a better place for everyone. The result is a document I named "The Bucket List Life Manifesto."

The Bucket List Life Manifesto has been downloaded & shared across the Internet by dozens of readers already. You can download your own free poster of this document on my website.

You are an adventurer. Every day is an opportunity to move closer to your dreams. Don't buy into the lie that someday is a good time for anything. It isn't. Take a step today, no matter how small, that relates to your life goals. **TRY** a new skill, a new food, a new destination, a new occupation, a new hobby, a new discipline, a new hangout. Take a risk. Embrace failure as your teacher. In your adventures show respect – for your surroundings, the people you encounter, yourself. **BE CURIOUS.** Ask lots of questions. Listen much. "Because I want to," is a fine reason for pursuing a goal. But you'll reach it even faster if you dig for a better "why." Be amazed by your own life. Be amazed in the quiet & the loud, in the big dreams realized and the small goals reached. **DARE** to be inventive. Only you get to decide what makes your life adventurous. No idea is too difficult or unreachable to be included on your list. Think "not yet" instead of "not at all." Put your bucket list in writing. Share it with those who love you. Cheer others on toward their dreams. Make memories. **SAVOR** the anticipation of a goal. Be spontaneous when you can, but plan often. Plan your next trip. Plan to take a class or work with an expert. Plan to see a concert or play. Plan to amaze yourself.

About the Author

Lara Krupicka loves living the bucket list life and encouraging others to do the same. Her own bucket list includes touring Tuscany, learning how to make the perfect pie crust, going to a movie on opening night, and taking a photography class so she can actually know how to use the  DSLR camera she and her husband own.

Lara's articles about bucket lists have been in publications as varied as the *LA Times*, *Houston Family* and *Bucket List Living Magazine*. Her online resource list of Bucket List Websites and Apps is noted on *National Geographic's* Intelligent Traveler blog and in the book *Take Your Marriage from Good to Great One Date at a Time* by Steve Pare. She also moderates the Family Bucket Lists Moms & Dads FaceBook group.

As a journalist, Lara writes regularly for regional parenting magazines across North America and internationally. In her four years as a writing professional she has seen her words reach over one million readers. Lara is a Toastmaster certified speaker, presenting to hundreds of people in moms' groups and at women's events about topics related to finding and pursuing one's dreams and making the most of everyday life.

Lara and her husband Mike are raising their three girls in the Western Suburbs of Chicago, where they find many opportunities for adventure (in between soccer games, disc golf tournaments and church events).

An Invitation to Connect

Do you like what you have read and want more? Are you interested in interacting with other moms (and dads) who are learning how to weave a bucket list in with family life? Are you wanting to keep tabs on new resources for documenting and living out your bucket list?

Then I hope you will connect with me online in one or more of these venues:

Blog
I write a blog about bucket list living and parenting. You can read my posts at www.larakrupicka.com. I share about adventures my family and I take. I review books, magazines and websites that help moms and families seize opportunities to learn, grow and explore (especially ones that help us all fulfill bucket list goals). And I talk about the ups and downs of being a mom in today's world. I hope you will stop by. If you do, leave a comment to introduce yourself!

FaceBook Group
If you are looking for inspiration and fellow explorers in the world of bucket lists and family life, why not join our Facebook group, Family Bucket Lists Moms & Dads? Most weeks I throw out a question or point out a site or destination for discussion. It is a friendly (non-competitive) group and you will find yourself quite welcome there. Just click on the button to request to join and I will add you to our number.

Twitter

I also Tweet regularly with bucket list sayings, links to sites and other adventure-related topics. And of course, parenting topics figure in there quite frequently too. If you are a Twitter user, why not follow me there (@amusingmom)? I am happy to follow back, especially if you note you found me through this book.

Pinterest

And if you want to see a visual representation of the latest and greatest ideas I have found related to bucket lists, particularly for moms, head on over to my Pinterest page (amusingmomlara). I have boards with bucket list sayings, ideas for commemorating your experiences, options for families, and much, much more. Pinterest is my favorite venue for all things bucket lists.

Check Out *Family Bucket Lists*

Family Bucket Lists: Bring More Fun, Adventure & Camaraderie Into Every Day
(2013, Wordcrafter Communications)

Do you have a list of "someday" things – a list of what you'd like to do or see, famous people you'd like to meet, roles you'd like to fill? A bucket list of goals for your lifetime?

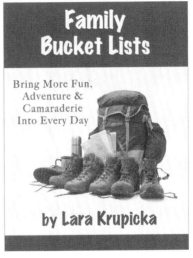

What if you combined that "someday" list with today's list of things "to do"? If you're thinking it sounds too expensive or would take too much time, think again. When you allow your bucket list to converge with everyday life, you'll find a whole host of benefits unfold in your life. And when you bring your family along... well, let's just say your life will never be the same.

Family Bucket Lists gives families a chance to:
- Dream together of what they want to do before the children are grown.
- Set off on adventures, big and small, together and individually.

- Enliven weekends and vacations with plans that match what they want most from life.
- Discover new things about one another as each person unearths and shares their dreams and aspirations.
- Find simple ways to incorporate life goals into everyday living.
- Make the most of the years they have together.

Parents who read *Family Bucket Lists* will be encouraged to:

- Honor themselves and their own their life goals now, even in the midst of raising children.
- Support their children in taking appropriate risks and trying new ventures.
- Let go of the desire to steer their children's paths and enjoy watching their children carve a path to the future.
- Define family fun according to their crew's unique bent.

Compiling bucket lists has given meaning and purpose to the free time my family has together. And it has allowed us to each find ways to cheer one other on in achieving goals (and understand where those desires are coming from). We're able to break long-term, seemingly impossible ideas down into manageable short-term events – and then live them out. And when one of us gets to accomplish a big dream, we all celebrate! There's nothing like living out our bucket lists here and now as a family.